Qumran and Corinth

QUMRAN

and

CORINTH

by

MARTIN H. SCHARLEMANN

BOOKMAN ASSOCIATES :: New York

Library of Congress Catalog Card Number: 62-10887

MANUFACTURED IN THE UNITED STATES OF AMERICA BY
UNITED PRINTING SERVICES, INC.
NEW HAVEN, CONN.

Foreword

AN EXAMINATION of the community at Qumran and the Christian Corinth on the basis of primary sources is here presented in the light of their sense of community, the eschatological hopes of each, and the responsibilities each assumed or shared before the coming of the Last Day. The study of parallel practices indicates a few possible interrelationships in the societal and religious life of two groups living in the centuries closest to the birth of Christ. The contrasts in organization, spheres of influence, and ideologies are evident. The purpose of the study is to throw more light on the letters of Paul to the Corinthians, particularly his first letter.

Scholarship of this kind, which gives greater insight into and added dimensions to the biblical record, makes a distinct contribution to the Christian community today. It enlightens the past and shows its relevance for the present. It points to a greater appreciation of the fellowship of the saints under Gospel, the Church, than is possible in a sectarian group under the Law. It therefore demands the serious attention of the Church as well as the world of scholars.

Graduate Study V takes its place alongside the previous studies to serve the Church and to glorify the Lord of the Church. Its author is professor of New Testament at Corcordia Seminary, a reservist chaplain of the Air Force with the rank of Colonel, a writer, essayist, and lecturer of note. As president of the Lutheran Academy for Scholarship he has played a leading role in promoting theological scholarship within The Lutheran Church—Missouri Synod.

CARL S. MEYER, *Director*
School for Graduate Studies
Concordia Seminary, St. Louis

Preface

In his *Ecclesiastical History* Eusebius discusses the work of Origen at some length, particularly the publication of his Hexapla. At that point he remarks: "At any rate, in the Hexapla of the Psalms, after the four well-known editions, he placed beside them not only a fifth but also a sixth and a seventh translation; and in the case of one of these he has indicated again that it was found at Jericho in a jar in the time of Antoninus the son of Severus" (VI, 16). Some five and a half centuries later the Nestorian Catholicos Timothy I wrote a letter to Mar Sargio, the Metropolitan of Elam, in which he noted that some trustworthy Jews, who were being instructed in the Christian faith, had told him of some books that had been found in the neighborhood of Jericho. An Arab had been out hunting one day, these converts were saying, when his dog followed its prey into a cave. Since the dog did not return, its master also entered the cave. He found it to be a small dwelling place containing many books.When he reported this to the Jews at Jerusalem, they came out and "found books of the Old (Testament) and others in Hebrew script."

Why were not these intriguing clues pursued, especially after Oscar Braun published Timothy's letter in 1901? Even as late as October 25, 1947, Millar Burrows, who has given us the most detailed description of the circumstances surrounding the discovery of the Dead Sea Scrolls, took John C. Trever and Wm. H. Brownlee, two Fellows

7

from the American School of Oriental Research at Jerusalem, on a trip to Kallia, proceeding from there to the
traditional site of the baptism of Jesus, without knowledge
of the importance of a cave that was within walking distance and had already yielded its treasures to certain
members of the Arab tribe of Tahamire.

It was quite by chance, as a matter of fact, that the
modern discoveries were made. It is not possible to piece
together all of the bits of information relating to the
discovery of the scrolls in what we now call Cave One.
Such details as are available have been taken from the
testimony of "Mohammed the Wolf," a fifteen-year-old
Arab boy, who was interrogated two years after the find.
According to this account, "The Wolf" was out looking for
a goat that had strayed from the herd. He was tired and
sat down in the shade of a hollow in the rock. To amuse
himself, he threw a stone into a hole in the cliff-face in
front of him. The sound of broken crockery sent him scur-
rying. The next day he brought with him one of his cousins. The two boys wormed their way through the hole
into the cave. At the back, beyond a floor strewn with
potsherds, they found eight jars. All but one were empty.
Out of this one, however, they recovered one large scroll
and two smaller ones.

Scrolls are not the kind of items that normally appeal
to shepherd boys. The cousins were disappointed and
wondered what to do with their find. Some weeks later,
one of their uncles brought all the scrolls taken from
this cave to a Bethlehem antiquities dealer, Khalil Eskan-
der, who was a member of the Syrian Orthodox community in that village. He in turn informed another merchant
belonging to their church at Jerusalem, George Isaiah; and

he in turn notified Mar Athanasius Yeshue Samuel, the Syrian Metropolitan-Archbishop, at the Monastery of St. Mark, on the theory that these were Syriac manuscripts.

Meanwhile clandestine excavations began in the cave, and other rolls, in more or less good condition, were recovered from the débris. In the fall of 1947, Bedouins and antique-dealers went from one learned institution to another in Jerusalem, offering their manuscripts at very reasonable prices. Mar Athanasius bought four: the Isaiah scroll, a *pesher* on Habakkuk, the *Manual of Discipline*, and another document which eventually turned out to be *A Genesis Apocryphon*. For the Hebrew University E. L. Sukenik purchased an imperfect copy of Isaiah, a collection of hymns, and the *Battle Scroll*.

As the situation in Palestine deteriorated toward the end of the British mandate, Mar Athanasius undertook to sell his manuscripts in the United States. He did not, however, find selling them on the American market as easy as he had hoped. It was not until 1955 that they were finally purchased for the Hebrew University by the State of Israel for the respectable price of $250,000.00.

Strangely enough the discovery of the next important cave (No. 4) was due to an incident strongly reminiscent of the huntsman's dog mentioned in the letter of Timothy I. While members of the Tahamire tribe were discussing their finds, an old man present recalled that years before he had followed a wounded partridge into a certain cave that was hard to reach. He made an effort to recall the details; and, on the basis of this information, some of the younger men of the tribe found the cave, not in the cliff-face skirting the Dead Sea, but dug into the side of the plateau nearer the Sea. To date eleven caves have been found. Their general condition is described in the essay proper. Only Cave 11 contained further scrolls, as distinct from fragments. No official account of the character of its contents has as yet been published, possibly because it has not yet been possible to purchase them from the Bedouins, who by this time know that, for some reason or other, Europeans and Americans are ready to pay a high price for such discoveries. Unofficial descriptions speak of two nearly complete copies of Daniel, a small scroll containing part of Leviticus in the ancient Hebrew script, a Targum of Job in Aramaic, a fine copy of the Psalter, and large fragments of the *Apocalypse of the New Jerusalem.*

We shall have to wait for official corroboration of these reports. Whatever else is found will not add much to our knowledge of the body of literature to which the scrolls belong. We are dependent for our current information on scrolls from Cave 1, on the many fragments from that and other caves, and on the previously known *Damascus Covenant.*

One may wonder why so much more is known of the Dead Sea Scrolls than of another significant discovery at Nag-Hammadi in Upper Egypt comprising the secret books of the Egyptian Gnostics. These documents were removed from a jar in Egypt at some time during 1945 or 1946 and constitute the finest batch of writings on religious subjects that the soil of this ancient land has yet yielded. But there was nothing so dramatic about their exhumation. Nearly everything took place behind the heavy curtains of cautious discretion. There was no journalist like Edmund Wilson to write up this Egyptian find, as he did in the case of the Dead Sea Scrolls in an article for the *New Yorker* in 1955. Another reason may be that the Dead Sea Scrolls are in fact more directly useful for our understanding of Scripture than the secret gospels are, since the latter date from a time after the books of our New Testament had been written.

The Qumran scrolls are important for an appreciation of the New Testament mostly because they were written not long before the birth of Jesus and also because they represent the literature of a religious community that was in actual existence in the days of our Lord—just a short distance, as a matter of fact, from the place where Jesus was baptized! Cullmann has gone so far as to suggest that the Hellenists mentioned in the early chapters of Acts were originally members of this Dead Sea sect. This position is somewhat difficult to maintain. Yet it would be strange if none of the earnest religious people of this community ever accepted Jesus, especially after their own way of life was destroyed.

The Dead Sea Scrolls, then, provide us with further background materials for our New Testament studies. This sect remained strictly within the confines of Judaism. The documents we have contain no traces of the cardinal doctrines of Christianity, such as the Incarnation, redemption through the Cross, the resurrection of the dead, the second coming of Jesus, or even the outpouring of the Holy Spirit. The members of this religious community considered themselves to be the remnant in Israel, bound to faithful obedience to the Law of Moses. They were determined to bring in the Kingdom as this was suggested to them by their understanding particularly of Isaiah 40.

There are a number of ways in which a comparative study of the Scrolls and the New Testament might have been undertaken. The present analysis is devoted to one aspect alone: the nature and content of religious fellowship. In the Pauline corpus no epistle devotes more space to this problem than does First Corinthians. That is why this epistle was chosen as the basis of a study in contrasts between the conception of *Gemeinschaft* held by the church and that of the Qumran sect. This study will serve to underline the distinctive features and dimensions of the church as Paul, the apostle, helped her to understand her mission in the world of the end-time. Our booklet goes forth in the hope that its content and method may serve as a contribution to a more profound awareness of the special heritage that is ours as members of the congregation of the end-time.

MARTIN H. SCHARLEMANN

The Day of St. Matthias, 1961.

Contents

Contents

Introduction

IN THIS ESSAY we propose to undertake a comparative study of the fabric of community life as it prevailed in the Qumran sect toward the end of its history and in the Corinthian church shortly after its founding. Such an analysis will provide the opportunity for observing not only the striking similarities but also the radical differences in the design of these two societies. At the same time it will furnish at least a partial answer to the question as to whether Christianity was little more than a kind of Essenism that made good.[1]

Though geographically separated by many miles, both Qumran and Corinth belonged to the Graeco-Roman world in the middle of the first century of our era. Both communities pursued religious ideals. Both owed much to the Old Testament and to Judaism in terms of vocabulary, concepts and convictions. To use St. Paul's figure, both "were grafted in their place to share the rich root of the olive tree."[2] To be sure, in terms of direct origins the Dead Sea sect had behind it a history of possibly two hundred years. Nevertheless, the literature from this group seems to reflect the conditions that prevailed in its life during the first century of the Christian era. That is one important reason for making this sect a proper subject of comparison with a church that was founded around 50 A.D.

On the surface of things, these two societies held similar views of history and of God's foreknowledge. A sense of divine destiny pervaded the faith of each group. Yet the contrasts between the two communities, in terms of hope and method, by far outweighed what they had in common. The Dead Sea sect was part of a larger group whose outlook was oriented to a life away from the world. Its members solemnly swore to be neither of the world nor in the world. They organized themselves very tightly under the discipline of the Law in order to achieve maximum ritual purity as a means of hastening the day of the Lord. The church in Corinth, on the contrary, was located in a vigorous and even licentious metropolis that served as a melting pot for the whole Mediterranean basin. Here the apostle Paul established a church to be in the world but not of it, to practice a new quality of life under the gift of God's Spirit, as its members awaited the consummation of the ages.

Both communities were persuaded that their respective existences constituted part of the end-time. Qumran went about its tasks on the principle of rigidly excluding anything unclean, fondly dreaming of a day when thousands of true Israelites would return from the "desert of the nations" to the wilderness of Judah for the final assault against the rule of Belial and his hosts. The church in Corinth vigorously reached out to gather in the Gentiles —especially when the doors of the synagogue were closed to it—on the conviction that this was part of the task of implementing the victory over Satan that had already been achieved at the resurrection of Jesus Christ. The former was organized as an army of priests concerned with problems of logistics, of *esprit de corps*, of rank, and of battle slogans; the latter, though comprising "not many that were wise, humanly speaking, not many that enjoyed prestige, not many that were well-bred" (1:26), found itself overwhelmed by an outpouring of the gifts of the Spirit so generous that the whole pattern of community life threatened to burst asunder in one mighty demonstration of personal liberty. For the one, our sources of information are some scrolls that remained buried and hidden for almost nineteen hundred years; for the other, we have the personal correspondence of the man who founded the community, epistles that have been read as living literature throughout these same centuries. Qumran ceased to exist when the Tenth Roman Legion overran the area as part of a campaign against Jerusalem, where stood the Temple of the Most High; the church at Corinth lives to this day, constituting part of the very temple of this living God.

In setting forth these similarities and contrasts we are, however, already anticipating some of the conclusions of this study. For that reason we must now deal with the design for community life at both Qumran and Corinth in terms of their pattern of continuity and discontinuity with the Old Testament. In this undertaking we shall consider the various documents which have come to light in recent years as they describe the organization and faith of the Dead Sea sect. In the instance of Corinth, our sources are of a different nature, consisting as they do of the personal letters of the apostle Paul. Our immediate interests will be limited primarily to what we know as First Corinthians, although Second Corinthians will be used to the extent that it becomes useful in determining certain specific aspects of our study.

Our presentation is divided into four major sections. The first one is devoted to the various terms and concepts used both at Qumran and by St. Paul to express their respective sense of community. In the second unit we propose to depict each of these societies in their conviction of being communities of the end-time. The third part will discuss the interim responsibilities each of these groups proposed to assume during the days before the final catastrophe of God's great judgment. The last portion describes the various dangers threatening the community design in each place.

Abbreviations

Chapter One

Expressing the Sense of Community

We proceed, then, to a study of the various words used at both Qumran and Corinth to articulate their respective convictions that the members constituted not merely an association but a true community. The circumstances connected with the writing of First Corinthians are too well known to require repetition here. The preface to the present study offers some of the background information for the Scrolls.

As things now stand, the literature from the Judean desert consists of three kinds of materials. The most ancient scrolls come from the caves in the vicinity of Wady Qumran. These date from the second century before our era to the first century after Christ. The documents from Murabba'at go back only to the time of the Second Jewish Revolt, while the materials found in the Byzantine monastery at Hirbet Mird were written in the fifth and sixth centuries of the Christian era. All of these literary remains of days long past will eventually be available in the monumental volumes of *Discoveries in the Judean Desert,* presently being edited by D. Barthélemy and J. T. Milik and published by the Clarendon Press at Oxford, England.

For our present purposes we are limiting ourselves to
the major items from Cave One and to what is often
known as the *Zadokite* or *Damascus Document*, found
by Solomon Schechter, toward the end of the last century,
in the Ezra synagogue at Old Cairo. All of these documents have been translated by various persons. In their
most convenient form they are to be found in Theodor
Gaster's *The Dead Sea Scriptures*, which is a paper-bound
Doubleday Anchor book. Our basic references in translation are to this volume. The Hebrew text for most of
these scrolls was published by the American Schools of
Oriental Research in 1950 and 1951 under the title, *The
Dead Sea Scrolls of St. Mark's Monastery*. There is a more
recent, pointed text, with a concordance, in Abraham
Haberman's *Megilloth Midbar Yehuda* (Tel Aviv, 1959).

This literature leaves us in no doubt whatsoever that
the Dead Sea sect thought of itself as a community. It
applied to itself the Hebrew term יחד, for example.
In fact, this word occurs in the very first line of the
Manual of Discipline, which is known as *Serek Hayahad*.
Basically יחד means "together." It is often used as an
adverb in Hebrew. If we were to translate the Hebrew
title of the Manual in a very literal way, we would need
to call it "The Practice of Togetherness." No title could
possibly underscore more heavily the sense of community
felt at Qumran, whose members thought of themselves
as the fellowship of God, היחד אל (1 QS 1:12).

Among the literary remains of Qumran there is a two-
column fragment known as *Serek Ha' edah*, which means
the "Rule of the Congregation." It contains a description
of the practices of the future community, when the whole
body of the true Israel "lead lives in the manner of the

sons of Zadok, the priests, and of those associated with them." The sect used the word עֵדָה of itself, too. The Manual speaks of the "assembly of holiness" (1 QS 5:20), for example. Another word for "assembly" is the Hebrew סוֹד. These sectarians referred to themselves as the "eternal assembly" (1 QS 2:25).

At this point we must take special note of the fact that this community did not normally speak of itself as the *qahal* of Yahweh, for which the Septuagint, as a rule, uses the phrase ἐκκλησία τοῦ θεοῦ. In fact, as far as our present literature is concerned, the term קָהָל, referring to the Qumran sect itself, occurs only in the description of the sixth standard, carried into battle by the army of the end-time. The inscription on this banner is to read קְהַל אֵל (1 QM 4:10), in distinction from the first one which carries the legend עֲדַת אֵל (1 QM 4:9). The only other occurrence of the word has reference to the hosts of the sons of darkness (1 QM 15:10). The significance of this failure to use a very common Old Testament term cannot be overrated; for it points to one of the essential differences between Qumran and Corinth. The Greek word ἐκκλησία was one with which the Gentile world had become very familiar. The Greeks had used it, and were still using it, as a matter of fact, of public assemblies. It occurs just in that sense three times in Acts 19 (vv. 32.39.41), where the reference is to the town assembly of Ephesus. This is the word on which the translators of the Septuagint had settled to render the Hebrew קָהָל, except for a small number of texts, where they used συναγωγή instead. This remarkable phenomenon—that is, the non-use of a very familiar Old Testament term—hints strongly at a fact to which we shall revert later on; namely, that Qumran thought of itself as the true people of God, the remnant in Israel; while the church of Corinth was taught to think of itself as the new Israel, gathering in the Gentiles as part of the task of the end-time.

At Corinth Christians felt a strong sense of community, too, despite their factionalism. In fact, it was the apostle's chief purpose in writing to this congregation to persuade them to give more adequate expression to the fact that God had specifically designed His church to be a *Gemeinschaft* rather than just a *Gesellschaft*, to use a distinction made popular in theology by the work of Dietrich Bonhoeffer.[3] Paul, therefore, addressed his epistle to the *ekklesia* of God, the one situated in Corinth (1 Cor. 1:2). Furthermore, Paul spoke of the members of this congregation as "brethren," a term used not only by the *thiasoi*, the religious associations familiar to the Greek world, but one that could be heard also among the *haburoth*, the theological fellowships of Judaism. According to the apostle's own convictions, the Corinthian church ought to think of itself as the body of Christ, a figure so bold as never to occur either in the Old Testament or in the literature of Qumran. In point of fact, this is not a figure of speech at all. It is neither allegory, nor metaphor, nor an analogy. It is a way of speaking about the most assured reality of the redemption that we have in Jesus Christ. That is why St. Paul spends so much time with this expression in chapter 12. It helped him in depicting the full dimensions of the relationship individual members in the church had toward each other just because they were, as the apostle put it, not a body of Christians, but the body of Christ Himself.

This sense of unity that each community, the one at

Corinth the other at Qumran, was expected to understand and appreciate is to be found also in the whole concept of *election*. This thought of God's choice of Israel was closely related to the establishment of God's covenant with His people. It bulks very large in the Old Testament and is most succinctly articulated in Deuteronomy 7:6-8:

> For you are a people holy to the Lord your God; the Lord your God has chosen you to be a people for his own possession, out of all the peoples that are on the face of the earth. It was not because you were more in number than any other people that the Lord set his love upon you and chose you, for you were the fewest of all peoples; but it is because the Lord loves you, and is keeping the oath which he swore to your fathers, that the Lord has brought you out with a mighty hand, and redeemed you from the house of bondage, from the hand of Pharaoh, king of Egypt. (Here see also Ezekiel 16:1-14.)

At Qumran the Gentiles and the unfaithful in Israel were referred to as people "whom God did not choose from eternity" (CD 2:7). By way of contrast God had chosen the remnant for an eternal covenant, so that theirs might be "all the glory of Adam" (1 QS 4:23). The *pesher* on Habakkuk (10:13) calls the Qumran members "the chosen of God" (בְּחִירֵי אֵל). They thought of themselves as the "chosen of the end-time" (1 QS 9:14) and as the "elect of His favor" (1 QS 8:6). It was, therefore, made incumbent on all members of the community "to love all that [God] has chosen" (1 QS 1:4).

The thought of God's choice of a people occurs rather frequently in the writings of the apostle Paul. He was able to add to the Old Testament truth of the election of a community of God's grace the new revelation that this

had taken place on the plane of history in the person of
Jesus Christ. St. Paul was fully aware of the fact that the
very center of God's self-disclosure was to be found in
His dealings with His people, with Israel in the days of
the old covenant, with the church in the present age of
fulfillment.

Now, the verbal adjective ἐκλεκτός does not occur in the
Corinthian correspondence. The verb, however, is used
three times in the following sentence (1 Cor. 1:27-29):
"God chose what is foolish in the world to shame the wise,
God chose what is weak in the world to shame the strong,
God chose what is low and despised in the world, even
things that are not, to bring to nothing things that are,
so that no human being might boast in the presence of
God." This passage certainly makes it unmistakably clear
that we are here dealing with a term which suggests that
the church came into being solely by divine initiative.
It is the application of our Lord's statement to the disciples, "You did not choose me, but I chose you" (John
15:16).

As a result of God's choice, Israel of old had become
His instrument for extending the knowledge of Yahweh
to the ends of the earth. The Dead Sea sect conceived
itself to be such a divine means of "effecting atonement
for the earth and ensuring the requital of the wicked"
(1 QS 8:6-7). That is why its members remained in the
desert awaiting the end of all things. They were sure that
"God would not exterminate His people by the hand of
the heathen, but would place the execution of judgment
on all the heathen in the hands of His elect" (1 QpHab
5:3,4). The church at Corinth, on the contrary, had been
created—of this St. Paul was very sure!—to reach out in

redemption for all, including the Gentiles. In fact, many
of the members of the church had been heathen, "led
astray to dumb idols, however you may have been moved,"
as St. Paul put it (1 Cor. 12:2). But now by the Spirit of
God, they could say, "Jesus is Lord" and share with their
Jewish brethren in the outpouring of a great variety of
spiritual gifts, bestowed on them to edify the whole congregation of God.

Another concept used by the Old Testament to refer
to Israel's liberation as a people from the house of bondage in Egypt is that of *calling*. The idea goes back to the
time when Abram was called and ordered to move to a
land that God would show him. Admittedly, the Old
Testament context, in Genesis 12, does not use קָרָא here;
but the Epistle to the Hebrews does, at 11:8: "By faith
Abraham obeyed when he was called to go out to a place
which he was to receive as an inheritance." This word is
applied specifically, in Hosea 11:1, to Israel, God's son,
as being called out of Egypt to inherit the Promised Land.

At Qumran the thought of choice and of calling occur
together, for example, in the Covenant of Damascus
(4:4): "By 'sons of Zadok' is meant those elect of Israel
that have been called by name and that shall go on functioning in the last days." The same document (2:11)
expresses the conviction that "in all their generations
[God] has ever raised up for himself persons called by
name" (קְרִיאֵי שֵׁם). The seventh battle standard listed
in the War Scroll (3:2) carries the inscription, "The
Called of God," which Gaster translates as "The Enlisted
of God," thereby blurring its theological significance.

St. Paul addressed the Corinthians as κλητοί right in the
salutation (1:2). The verb itself occurs several times. Its

communal overtones can be heard very clearly in chapter one, verse nine, for example: "God is faithful, by whom you were called into the fellowship of His Son. . . ." Very significantly, this term is applied to the station of life into which the individual has been called. "Only, let every one lead the life which the Lord has assigned to him," says St. Paul (7:17), "and in which God has called him. This is my rule in all the churches." This usage points to a basic difference between Qumran and Corinth. No one at Corinth was asked to leave the city and repair to a desert place for a life of ritual purity. On the contrary, each member of the church was to serve as a Christian right where he was. The apostle put it like this: "So, brethren, in whatever state each was called, there let him remain with God" (7:24). That is to say, each member was to live in his calling, not as an isolated Christian, but as one who belonged to the new community, the church.

Possibly this last point needs a little emphasis in our day, which suffers so much from the blight of individualized Protestantism. One of the church fathers used to say, "*Unus Christianus, Nullus Christianus.*" Applying this observation to our present context, it would mean that St. Paul thought of each Christian at Corinth as carrying out the responsibilities of his particular job in society by remaining fully aware of the fact that he was serving there as one who belonged to another order, the church of God. That is to say, the consciousness of belonging to a newly created community was to pervade the life of the individual in all of his relationships.

St. Paul often used the term "called" in combination with ἅγιοι "saints," or "holy one." He does so in the salutation of each of the two letters to Corinth. Six times in

First Corinthians he calls Christians οἱ ἅγιοι, including the intriguing passage in chapter six (2a): "Or don't you know that the saints will judge the world?" This is followed in the next verse with the question, "Do you not know that we are to judge angels?"

The use of this word reflects the Old Testament understanding of קָדוֹשׁ. In its application to Israel, one of the crucial passages on this point is Exodus 19:6: "And you shall be to me a kingdom of priests and a holy nation." Holiness properly belongs to God. Of this the Old Testament authors are very sure. It was given to Israel as this people was set aside for service to God.

The idea of separation inherent in holiness pervades the literature of Qumran. The members of the sect are known as "the people of an holy covenant" (1 QM 10:10) and as "men of holy perfection" (1 QS 8:20). In fact, in the period of the final conflict, the priests of the community are instructed to give their orders at a distance from the battle lines so as not "to defile the oil of their priestly anointment with the blood of vain heathen" (1 QM 9:7-8). Sanctification in the community was achieved by immersion, which normally took place before the common meal, as Josephus pointed out in saying, "After the purification, they assemble in a special room which none of the uninitiated is permitted to enter; pure now themselves, they repair to the refectory, as to some sacred shrine."[4]

St. Paul's interest in washing by water was a sacramental one, likened to the experience of Israel at the Red Sea (10:2). Possibly, it is worth noting that the apostle's main statement on this matter occurs at the end of a major ethical section. At chapter six, verse eleven, he wrote: "But you were washed, you were sanctified,

you were justified in the name of the Lord Jesus Christ
and in the Spirit of our God." This is the indicative of
God's action toward the Corinthian Christians. From this
there followed the imperative of Christian living. That is
to say, in baptism God had created a new quality of life.
This was His gift to the church. Its members were to live
accordingly.

The implication of unity contained in the concept of
"holy ones" is clearly set forth in the Qumran Manual of
Discipline (11:7,8), which says, "God has given them an
inheritance in the lot of the holy beings and joined them
in communion with the angels, to form one congregation,
one single communion, a structure of holiness, an eternal
planting for all time to come." There are a half dozen
different expressions in just this one sentence to stress the
idea of oneness among those who were known as saints.

Two of these phrases deserve particular attention at
this point, because they occur in First Corinthians with
reference to the church. The first of these is "structure
of holiness," for which the Hebrew is מבנית קודש. The
community at Qumran was also designated as a "house
of holiness" (1 QS 8:5). This is elaborated in the next
column (9:5.6) as follows: "At the time, the men of the
community will constitute a true and distinctive temple—
a veritable holy of holies—wherein the priesthood may
fitly foregather, and a true and distinctive synagogue
made up of laymen who walk in integrity." In much the
same way St. Paul spoke of the Christians at Corinth as
being God's building (3:9) and as the temple of God
(3:16). In fact, he relates the thought of the temple to
that of holiness, when he says, in 3:17b: "For God's temple is holy, and that temple you are."

Into this kind of language we must also put the figure of the stone as it occurs especially in Isaiah 28:16. The Manual of Discipline specifically alludes to this passage in the statement (8:6): "They will be, indeed, a 'tested bulwark' and 'a precious cornerstone,' which shall never be shaken or moved from their place." Now, to be sure, St. Paul does not, in First Corinthians, use either *lithos* or *petra* in this particular sense. In chapter ten (v.4), the rock is the one from which the Israelites drank in the wilderness, here identified with Christ; and in chapter three the term "stones" occurs only in a sentence that describes the Christian life in terms of a building operation (v.12). However, in Romans 9:33, very likely written from Corinth, this very passage from Isaiah is used with specific reference to Christ and by implication of the church as God's new community.

The other concept conjoined with holiness at Qumran was that of an "eternal planting." The community, says the Manual (8:4), is a "plant evergreen." Here is a figure that had become familiar in Israel particularly since the days of Isaiah, who proclaimed (5:7): "For the vineyard of the Lord of hosts is the house of Israel, and the men of Judah are his pleasant planting." In point of fact, the idea of the people as a building and as a plant goes all the way back to the Song of Moses in Exodus 15:17, where we have the lines:

> Thou wilt bring them in, and plant
>   them on Thine own mountain,
> the place, O Lord, which Thou hast
>   made for Thine abode,
> the sanctuary, O Lord, which Thy
>   hands have built.

Both concepts occur together in First Corinthians (3:9), where St. Paul makes the point, "You are God's husbandry, God's building."

This temple, or this plant, the Qumran sect conceived to be one with the angels, as we have already seen in a previous quotation from the Manual (11:7.8). One of the hymns expresses this thought as follows (3:20): "For, lo, Thou hast taken a spirit distorted by sin, and purged it of the taint of much transgression, and given it a place in the host of the holy beings, and brought them into communion with the sons of heaven."[5] In passing, one ought to be permitted to ask whether some such thought of unity between the church and the angels lies behind that strange remark of St. Paul's in 1 Corinthians 11:10: "That is why a woman ought to have a veil on her head, because of the angels."

From this point, we must proceed to consider the term used in the New Testament for "fellowship," "communion." The Greek word is κοινωνία. In the New Testament κοινωνοί are persons who hold property in common. They are partners or shareholders in a common concern, as the sons of Zebedee were business partners with Simon (Lk. 5:10). Church members, for one thing, share the Gospel with each other. St. Paul, therefore, can say, as he does in 1 Corinthians 9:23: "I do it all for the sake of the Gospel, that I may share [with others, as the context clearly shows] in its blessings." The familiar phrase "fellowship of the Holy Spirit," consequently, is rendered by the Revised Standard Version as "participation in the Holy Spirit."

This partnership finds its expression in Christians sharing their money and their goods with one another. Such action represents no mere pooling of resources. For the church is not an association of separately living parts. The life that is shared exists only as shared. The services rendered by Christians to each other are not contributions out of their own resources; they are gifts to the church from God and are held for its benefit by the individual as a shareholder. The special embodiment of κοινωνία is to be found in the Lord's Supper, which is a sharing together in the body and blood of Christ. This is stated in 1 Corinthians 10:16-17: "The cup of blessing which we bless, is it not a participation in the blood of Christ? The bread which we break, is it not a participation in the body of Christ?"

In the literature of Qumran there is no term quite like that of κοινωνία. The idea is expressed rather by the word "sons" as in the phrase "sons of an everlasting communion" (בְּנֵי סוֹד עוֹלָמִים) (1 QS 2:25). But there can be no question at all of the fact that these sectarians practiced a partnership with each other. They were persons who had separated themselves "from the congregation of perverse men to become a community in Torah and in property" (1 QS 5:1-2). The concept of full fellowship was articulated as follows (1 QS 2:24): "All of them will thus be members of a community founded at once on true values and on a common sense of humility, on charity and mutual fairness—members of a society truly hallowed, partners in an everlasting communion."

Their sharing included that of material things. Qumran practiced a community of goods even more rigid than that of the early church, as we shall see later. Its members partook of a common meal which was thought of as a type of the Messianic banquet, when the Messiah of Aaron "is to pronounce the blessing over the first portion of the bread and wine" and the anointed king, the lay Messiah, is to follow him in stretching out his hand to the bread. "After that the members of the community in general are to pronounce the blessing in order of rank (1 QSa 2:19 ff).[6]

The community was presumably founded by the Teacher of Righteousness, who is described as the "priest in whose heart God put understanding to explain all the words of his servants the prophets" (1 QpHab 2:8-9). Accordingly, the Qumran group is sometimes designated as a community which is dedicated to the truth of a very special revelation. In one of the hymns, for example, the poet exclaims, "Thou hast made known to me Thy deep, mysterious things" (1 QH 4:27-28). And the song of the initiants, at the end of the Manual, includes the statement:

> For He from the Wellspring of Knowledge
> has made His light to burst forth,
> and mine eye has gazed on His wonders;
> and the light that is in my heart
> has pierced the deep things of existence (1 QS 11:3).[7]

From all of these phrases and concepts, used at Qumran and contained in St. Paul's letters to Corinth, it is evident to what extent and in what way these two communities were to think of themselves in terms of unity and community. We have also noted how this belief in being God's elect people took on a somewhat different significance in each of the two groups. It is time now to take up their persuasion that they were constituted as communities of the end-time.

Chapter Two

As Communities of the
End-Time

The literature of the Qumran sect leaves us in no doubt whatsoever that this community thought of itself as living in the last days of history. In doing so, the desert fellowship expressed its faith in terms of a time-scheme that had impressed its pattern on Jewish thought as a whole. It consisted of making a distinction between "this age" and "the age to come." Here was one way in which the group expressed its continuity with the Israel of the Old Testament. In fact, it was fully persuaded that its members constituted the true Israel. Accordingly it did not hesitate to refer to itself as "Israel." This is clear from the following passage in the Manual of Discipline (9:3): "When these things obtain in Israel, as defined by these provisions, the Holy Spirit will indeed rest on a sound foundation."

Moses and the prophets, therefore, were accepted as the sources of authority for the regulations of the sect. The Old Testament was regularly quoted and interpreted at length in various commentaries. Furthermore, those who wanted to join the community had to declare their willingness at once to do what was right in accordance with what God had "commanded through Moses and through his servants, the prophets" (1 QS 1:2). Hence,

35

the observance of the Sabbath and of other Jewish festivals was a primary responsibility. In point of fact, the rules pertaining to the Sabbath were more strictly binding out here in the desert than in Judaism as such. This is clear from the section devoted to this subject in what is known as the Zadokite or Damascus Document (10:14-11:18), which goes so far as to forbid lifting a new-born animal out of a cistern or pit on the Sabbath. The rigor of this prohibition certainly exceeds the implication of Luke 14:5 that this kind of work was not forbidden by the scribes. There we read of Jesus: "And he said to them, 'Which of you, having an ass or an ox that has fallen into a well, will not immediately pull him out on a sabbath day?' "

A very rigorous interpretation of the Mosaic Law was rather characteristic of Qumran, which considered itself to be the faithful remnant just because it demanded so much by way of moral achievement and ritual observance. As such it was sure that it served as God's instrument of salvation and of judgment, not only in the case of the heathen but also in the instance of the wicked among God's own people. It assumed the task of effecting atonement for the earth (1 QpHab 1:3-4).

At this point we are introduced to the thought of discontinuity in the faith of Qumran. Its members were persuaded that Israel in general had gone astray, and that, therefore, the faithful really had no choice except to separate themselves from the Jewish community in general. The Damascus covenant, therefore, interpreted the reference to the priests, the Levites, and the sons of Zadok in Ezekiel 44:15 as follows: "By 'priests' is meant those in Israel that repent and depart from the land of Judah. By 'levites' is meant those that associate themselves with them. By 'sons of Zadok' is meant those elect of Israel that have been designated by name and that shall go on functioning in the last days" (CD 4:2-4).[8]

This desert community followed a calendar of its own. This, too, was part of its pattern of discontinuity with the Old Testament. The members of this desert group were convinced that the dates on which the holy days were observed at the Temple in Jerusalem were "those in which all Israel was in error" (CD 3:14). This use of another kind of calendar was one of the reasons for separating from the nation as such. For, obviously, people who must observe religious feasts on days other than those of the community at large find it rather awkward to live with their fellow men.[9] This desert group was sure that it was observing the holy days of Israel according to a calendar that served as part of a new wisdom, revealed by God to make it possible to undo the errors that had originated with the fall of the angels (CD 2:18). Here we have an allusion to an idea that also occurs in the Book of Enoch,[10] according to which these evil angels had given to men the secrets of the lunar period.[11]

The members of Qumran did not worship at the Temple. The sect thought of itself and its life as being the equivalent of the sacrificial ritual that characterized the services in Jerusalem. This is one reason why priests figure so prominently in the sect. Its members referred to the community as a Holy of Holies, a true and distinctive temple of priests and a synagogue of laymen, as we have already seen. In such contexts these sectarians did not hesitate to call themselves "sons of truth," "sons of light," or "men of holy perfection." They were sure that they constituted the true remnant both in succession to and in distinction from Israel as such.

Turning now to Corinth, we can say that the church's pattern of continuity and discontinuity with ancient Israel is a particularly prominent feature of I Corinthians 10. There the apostle referred to the Israelites that had left Egypt as "our fathers" (v.1). What had occurred at the Red Sea and in the desert was interpreted typologically when, for example, Paul asserted that Christ had already dwelt in ancient Israel by means of the rock that accompanied them through the desert. He understood the church to stand in continuity with the people of the old covenant. The Old Testament, therefore, was quoted and cited as authoritative for the church. As Israel had been baptized at the Red Sea so Christians were now brought into the end-time people of God by baptism. As God's former *qahal* had been exposed to many trials and testings, so the church and its members had to endure the temptations of the end-time.

Despite all these similarities Paul felt a strong sense of discontinuity with Israel of old. The Law of Moses had been superseded by the presence of the living Lord as the final revelation from God. The old Israel was not willing to acknowledge this new Torah; hence Judaism, according to Paul, constituted the "Israel according to the flesh," preferring to remain bound to its system of physical sacrifices and ritual observances. The church, however, was the community of God's Spirit, who was himself the gift of the end-time. His presence produced a new quality of life in the church at Corinth. Its essence was freedom understood as service to God in any and every walk of life. This feeling of discontinuity expressed itself in particular by the substitution of the first day of the week for the Sabbath of the old covenant.

Qumran and Corinth thought of themselves as eschatological communities. Both were sustained by a strong faith that the end of the ages was near at hand. The Qumran doctrine of the end was closely connected with its belief in a cosmic dualism, according to which God had created both the Prince of Light and the Angel of Darkness. The hostility of these two toward each other pervaded all of life and would eventually bring on the final conflict. That this sect was passionately anticipating the end is clear from the interpretation put on Habakkuk 2:3 (1 Qp Hab 7:10-14): "This refers to the men of truth, the men who carry out the Law, who do not relax from serving the truth even though the final moment be long drawn out. Assuredly, all the times appointed by God will come in due course, even as he has determined in his inscrutable wisdom."[12] The very words of a passage like this indicate to what extent the coming of the end, particularly its delay, constituted a problem for the members of this group. The community believed that the Teacher of Righteousness, who was quite possibly the founder of the sect, had received a special revelation which enabled him to interpret the events of his day as being those of the last age.

Just precisely what segment of history he was interpreting is not clear from the commentaries we have. Some scholars are of the opinion that the revelation dealt with the period of the Seleucid kings; others just as vehemently defend the position that these commentaries were intended to illuminate the events of the Roman period of occupation. Be that as it may, the documents reflect a strong faith that God had now made known things which until then had been hidden to men. In fact, the *pesher* on the book of Habakkuk (1 Qp Hab 7:1-2) says in so many words that the prophet himself did not understand the full significance of his own predictions.[13] A new insight into the words of God's ancient prophet had been given within recent years to the new community. To be sure, the group still expected the coming of *the* Prophet, and the Messiahs of Aaron and of Israel (1 QS 9:11). There was every indication, however, that these men were to come very soon. On their arrival there would take place the final conflict between the sons of light and the sons of darkness. Then would come the moment when the sons of light "that were now in exile will return from the 'desert of the nations' to pitch camp in the desert of Jerusalem" (1 QM 1:3). This would be the time when those who had cast their lot with God would come to dominion, and those that had chosen the side of Belial would be doomed to eternal extinction. The members of the Qumran sect were in no doubt whatsoever as to the outcome of this final battle of a running cosmic conflict. The roster of those who would fight on God's side was already known in Heaven (1 QM 12:2). In fact, God Himself would muster the army of His elect, "in their thousands and tens of thousands," to fight side by side with His holy angels. Light would then become victorious over darkness. This conviction must have been a source of great comfort; for the community apparently never numbered more than a few hundred members. Its members were sustained by this vision of the future. Their hope was so strong that they did not hesitate to compose a hymn of victory in anticipation of their final but certain triumph.

We must note, in this connection, that the precise distinction between the end and the present moment is not always clearly drawn in the documents. That is to say, we cannot always be sure whether this community thought of the period in which it was then living as already constituting a part of the end or whether the end marked an entirely new period either within or beyond history. Faith often does not bother to be too specific in such matters. At any rate, only extermination without survival awaited the heathen and those in Israel who had been disloyal to the covenant; they would be destroyed by fire from the rivers of Belial (1 QH 3:29). These streams are pictured as about to flow through the world to consume everything. The following lines from the hymn referred to describe the moment:

When with his mighty roar
    God thunders forth,
And His holy welkin trembles
Through dread of his glory,
And the hosts of heaven give
    forth their voice,
And the world's foundations
    rock and reel;
When warfare waged by the soldiers
    of heaven
Sweeps through the world
    and turns not back until the final doom—
Warfare the like of which has never been (1 QH 3:34-36).[14]

In anticipation of this final catastrophe and in preparation for bringing in the kingdom of God, the community was organized as a kind of salvation army. The hosts that would fight at the side of this army in the future are carefully described in the War Scroll. Even the inscriptions

on the banners of various units are spelled out to the last
letter, each one suggesting the specific function of every
single command in the coming Armageddon.

We turn now to the church at Corinth. The apostle
wanted it to be motivated by a strong eschatological conviction. As far as Paul was concerned, the end was expected momentarily. "The appointed time has grown very
short," he wrote (7:29). He was probably quoting from
the early liturgy of the church in his reference to the
prayer, "*Marana tha*" (16:23).[15] The whole community
was expected to look forward with eager anticipation to
the end of all things. Some of the counseling on marriage
given in First Corinthians is based on the belief that the
Lord would return very shortly. This is why Paul saw no
reason for anyone to want to change his vocation. He
expressed a wish, furthermore, that people might remain
unmarried, as he himself was, so that they might live
among men as persons who served their needs but remained unencumbered by the affairs of this world. Christians were to prepare themselves for the consummation
of all things.

However, there is one great difference between the
hope of the Qumran community and that of the Corinthian
church. The church was founded on the conviction that
the Messiah had already come in the person of Jesus
Christ. He had been crucified and had risen from the
dead. This Paul makes unmistakably clear. The end of
time would come at His return, not again in grace, but in
judgment. The church, in other words, lived between the
two advents. This marked a new interpretation of time
and of history. For in the thinking of the apostle the final
victory over all of God's enemies had already been

achieved in the resurrection of Jesus. All that now remained was the subjection of the remaining enemies of
his Lord (15:25-28). The church, therefore, actually lived
in the end-time.

This meant that any history yet to come found its
meaning for the church in the expanding conquests of
the Messiah. He was even now the Lord of the universe,
who had ascended to the right hand of the Father. The
last enemy to be overcome would be death itself. At his
complete subjection Christ would return the rule to His
Father so that God might be all in all.

The consummation of all things would be accompanied
by the final judgment, when everyone, including the apostle himself, could expect the Lord's verdict on what he
had done. The Lord would expose the secrets of men's
hearts to the consuming fire of judgment. Whatever had
lasting value would survive the crisis of this final catastrophe (3:13-15).

From our analysis of the motivating hope of each of
these two communities, we must now turn to a consid-
eration of the means by which individuals became members of these respective groups. Not everyone belonged
either to the Qumran sect or to the church at Corinth.
There was a prescribed method of entering the fellowship of each.

The faith of the desert sect is most clearly set forth in
the third and fourth columns of the Manual of Discipline.
This doctrinal section opens with the invitation to "the
enlightened one" that he instruct his fellows in the *tola-
doth* of all the sons of men. That is to say, the instructor
was to set forth all that happens to mankind in the light
of God's foreknowledge, and of the division among men

into sons of light and children of darkness. In short, predestination, dualism, and eschatology constituted the subject matter of instruction at Qumran.[16]

The young children in the community had to undergo a ten-year period of training. They studied a manual specifically designed for this purpose. It dealt with the provisions and requirements of the covenant. Not until their twentieth year were children eligible for membership. When a person was otherwise ready to become a member of the community, he was examined publicly regarding his intellectual capacity and his moral character. If he passed this test, he was required to submit himself to a year's probation. At this point he was not yet admitted to the common table; nor did he have a share in the resources of the community. At the end of his novitiate he came up again for review. If he was considered to be qualified, he had to serve another year on probation. At this stage of his training he was obliged to place all property in trust with an overseer. He, himself, however, was not yet permitted to dine with the members of the community; nor did he have the privilege of having a share in their materials and supplies. He could become fully enrolled only after this second year of training, and then only by a general vote of the whole assembly and after swearing an oath of allegiance.

Once he became a full member he was reckoned as belonging to the *rabbim,* a word applied to God's elect. The commentary on Habakkuk uses this same term of kings and rulers, in the sense of "great ones." This is of some significance as we consider the church at Corinth. For part of the difficulty of this church, as St. Paul describes it, arose from the conviction of some of the members, at least, that they were already kings, that they were living beyond eschatology, so to speak (cf. 4:7.8). Now, it is just possible that this strange idea came to Corinth by way of Apollos, whom Acts 18. 24-28 describes as having belonged to the movement begun by John the Baptist. It is possible that John, for a time at least, lived in the Qumran community.[17] In the Gospel of Luke we read that he lived in desert places (1:80). After the death of his aged parents, he may have been adopted by the community; for we know that this was the practice of the Qumran sect.[18] It is clear, however, from the information the Gospels give us that John did not share the conviction of the sect that the community of the end-time was to be established in the desert of Judah. He himself turned in his proclamation to the task of sending men back from the wilderness into the world to carry on their work there in the light of a new faith. To this point we shall return at the end. We mention it here only to suggest that there is some likelihood that Apollos, before he received further training from Aquila and Priscilla, carried something of this idea of the present dominion of God's elect to the church at Corinth, and that this notion persisted even after he himself had changed his point of view.

We can conclude from First Corinthians that the apostle, and presumably also the local prophets and teachers, engaged in instruction to prepare people for intelligent membership in the church. This is evident, for example, from the opening verses of Chapter 15, where Paul uses the technical terms for teaching and learning. There he gives a brief summary of the content of this instruction in such a way as to suggest an early creedal formulation, namely, that "Christ died on behalf of our sins and that he was buried, and that he was raised on the third day, according to the Scriptures, and that he appeared to Cephas, then to the Twelve." This matter of instruction is mentioned even earlier, in connection with the establishment of the Lord's Supper as the sacred meal of the new covenant. An examination of the words of institution will reveal that the teaching done by the church through its proper persons must have included a rather thorough discussion of the Old Testament in terms of the pattern of continuity and discontinuity. This task was made easier for the church by the fact that many of its members had previously belonged to the synagogue, either as full members or as proselytes. There they had become accustomed to hearing the Law and the prophets read and expounded by qualified individuals. In addition, a Greek translation of the Old Testament, known as the Septuagint, had given the Roman world access to the sacred treasures of Israel's scriptures. Nevertheless, instruction in the faith of the church required the same kind of radical reorientation that Paul himself experienced at his conversion. For admission into the church was attained by way of baptism, when each candidate had to confess that Jesus was Lord,[19] with all that this implied for an understanding of life and history.

The church at Corinth did not prescribe any period of probation. Baptism was a divine act of liberation from the Egypt of ignorance, immorality and idolatry. It was a recapitulation, so to speak, of Israel's baptism in the waters of the Red Sea (10:2). In fact, by this rite each new member of the church became part of a people whose history reached back to the Exodus, as the observance of

the passover, now turned into Easter, was sure to remind
the Corinthians (5:7.8).

The very fact that the apostle relates the church's baptism so closely to Israel's earliest history, at the Sea of
Reeds and in the desert, indicates to what extent the
whole story of Israel's creation constituted a part of the
instruction given for church membership. In this respect
we note a striking similarity between Corinth and Qumran. For also in the desert of Judah the priests were "to
recount the righteous acts of God in his many works and
tell of all the acts of steadfast love and mercy shown
toward Israel" (1 QS 1:20-21). There, however, the comparison between the two comes to an end. For the ablutions practiced by the Dead Sea sect were in reality
quite unlike Christian baptism. The thought of radical
liberation and re-creation does not seem to have been
associated with ritual bathing at Qumran. The interests
of this sect centered in continuous ceremonial purity.
Christian baptism, by way of contrast, was administered
only once in a lifetime as a means of rebirth from one
way of life to another. To be sure, the Manual of Discipline is quite specific in saying that anyone who does
not submit to the full discipline of the community "cannot be . . . cleansed by any waters of ablution nor sanctified by immersion in lakes or rivers or purified by any
bath" (3:4-5). Yet this very system of discipline rested
almost entirely on the concept of ceremonial cleanliness,
which necessarily required a great deal of bathing, as
Josephus points out in his description of the Essenes.[20]
There can be little doubt, therefore, that these ablutions
were not intended to signify the kind of total renewal

expressed, for instance, in that statement of the apostle to which we alluded in the first section: "But you were washed, you were sanctified, you were justified by the name of the Lord Jesus Christ and by the Spirit of our God" (6:11). To live according to the name of the Lord Jesus involved not only a new dimension to life but a complete break with one's past in the interest of total commitment to Jesus as Lord. Here was to be found the major significance of the baptismal confession of faith. At Qumran, by way of contrast, separation for service was accomplished by departing for the desert on the basis of individual decision, not by regeneration, through a sacramental action on God's part.

Chapter Three

Interim Responsibilities

We have seen to what extent and in what way both Qumran and Corinth were motivated by a strong conviction that they were communities of the end-time. At this point we must see how each of these two communities thought of their respective responsibilities while they were awaiting the consummation of the ages. The very expectation that the end was at hand made it incumbent on both groups to be prepared at all times to meet the demands of the final emergency. But how did the members of each carry on from day to day as they looked forward to the end? First of all, we must look at this question in terms of the way in which life was organized in each of these two communities. We have enough information in the documents under discussion to determine the general pattern of each. Again, we will discover certain similarities as well as contrasts between the two.

The community at Qumran determined to carry out its interim responsibilities, in part, by means of very rigid organization. Since it thought of itself as a priestly congregation, supreme authority in all doctrinal matters was vested in the priests, assisted by an order of levites. To be sure that doctrinal conclusions could be effectively imposed, the priests also decided the basic economic policies and practices of the sect. The general council, to which any members of the congregation in good standing might be elected, served as a deliberative body. It considered matters of general policy, including those of admission, promotion and demotion. For purposes of administration, there was also a kind of presbytery, consisting of three priests and twelve qualified laymen. Every member of the community was assigned a special rank, which came up for review each year. The basic operational unit in the life of the community consisted of ten men, one of whom had to be a priest. The latter had the task of leading others in matters of law and doctrine.

All the members of the community dined together, the food being first blessed by a priest. Everyone sat in order of rank or class, the priest occupying the first place at all times. The constituency met regularly for prayer and study. In fact, members were obliged to spend one-third of all the nights of the year in this kind of spiritual exercise. All the property belonging to individual members was placed in a common pool and was administered by an overseer. A similar officer presided over the allocation of communal tasks and duties. There are numerous references in the documents to a process of admission to or rejection from "the purity." This expression, in its various contexts, would seem to signify the different degrees or levels of ceremonial cleanliness ascribed to various strata within the total group. Josephus, incidentally, mentions four such degrees among the Essenes;[21] and it may well be that this was the precise pattern in force at Qumran.

In passing, it might be noted that the emphasis of this sect was on rank. Its members were seated at the common meal and in their assemblies according to their individual prerogatives. Their time to speak in the assembly was determined on this basis. At Corinth, by way of contrast, the apostle insisted on the principle of subordination. That is to say, in this new community, known as the church, each member was expected to be more concerned with the priority of others than with his own rights. As a matter of fact, the implication of Paul's insistence on this point is that in the church the individual really has no rights which he is free to exercise on the basis of rank. Instead, he has the responsibilities of concern for and service to others in terms of their needs. The apostle went so far as to apply this principle of subordination to the relationship of Jesus Christ to His Father in their common task of guiding history through its full course (15:27.28).

The Qumran community drew up a blueprint for the final campaign against the forces of Belial. This document is known as the War Scroll. It describes a priestly army devoted to its ceremonial duties under the guidance of the fathers of the community, fifty-two in number. The assembly itself had the responsibility of selecting soldiers for service in various foreign countries. To use the precise wording of the document, "They [the members of the assembly] are to draft them annually out of all the tribes of Israel in accordance with the established conventions of warfare" (1 QM 2:7-8). Even a cavalry is listed as part of the forces to be drawn up for the final attack against the sons of darkness.

In Corinth the church was sustained by the conviction that the decisive battle had been won. To use a very familiar figure of speech from Oscar Cullmann,[22] "D-day" lay in the past; the future was sure to usher in "V-day." An interval of time still remained to be reckoned with.

Yet each day led inevitably toward the end of all things, the triumph of the Lord's anointed.

The church in Corinth is described as coming under prophetic direction for its life. Paul reminded his readers that God had given to the new community apostles, prophets and teachers, in that particular sequence, in order to guide the church, endowed as it was with power to do miracles and heal the sick, to assist those who were in need, to administer church affairs, and even to speak in tongues. Its members regularly assembled for the *agape*, the *common meal*, which was followed by the celebration of the Eucharist. At these gatherings they were asked not to display their rank or wealth, but rather to devote their resources to taking care of the poor. They had been created as a community whose calling it was to manifest that love toward others which God had shown toward them in his redemptive activity. In this way they were to serve as priests. That is why, in Second Corinthians, the work of supplying the needs of the saints is actually called a *liturgy* (9:12).

Furthermore, order was to prevail in the public meetings of the congregation. As at Qumran, no one was to interrupt the previous speaker. However, in observance of the principle of subordination, anyone who spoke was under obligation to yield to the prophetic insight or revelation imparted to another (14:29), lest the charismatic gift of the Spirit be frustrated. Everything was to be done for the edification of the total group. On this basis the apostle forbade the speaking in tongues, unless an interpreter was present (14:28). Such a fundamental note of concern for the spiritual growth of the community as a whole is lacking almost entirely in the literature from Qumran.

That the congregation at Corinth as such had responsibilities for certain decisions seems to be implied by the apostle's reference (16:2) to persons accredited by the Christians of Corinth to forward monies gathered by way of freewill offerings for the poor "saints" in Jerusalem. This is also inherent in the apostle's direction to assemble for the purpose of delivering a man guilty of incest to Satan "for the destruction of the flesh, that his spirit may be saved in the day of the Lord" (5:5). Again, the members of the church at Corinth were not to take their problems in law into pagan courts. Such matters were to be adjudicated within the congregation itself on the principle that some day they would judge the world and even angels (6:1-3). We might note in this connection a similar attitude at Qumran. For instance, turning a member over to a pagan court for capital punishment was itself regarded as a heinous offense.

Despite the fact that among the skeletons found in the cemetery at Hirbet Qumran the remains of a few women could be identified, it is obvious that women did not play a part in the community life of the desert comparable to that of women in the early church at Corinth. Among its ideals the Dead Sea sect left very little room for married life, although it should be noted in this connection that there was a difference on this point between the covenanters at Damascus and the group for whom the Manual of Discipline was intended. The latter led a monastic kind of life, withdrawn from the world, at a place regulated by strict ascetic rules designed to achieve ritual purity, while the former drew up specific rules for family life.

At Corinth, the apostle found himself confronted by various problems related to the institution of marriage and the part women were to play in the life of the church as the community of the end-time. He was persuaded that the eschatological situation required the utmost in self-discipline, including celibacy (7:26). At the same time, however, he was realistic enough to recognize the desirability and even the necessity of getting married, except in the instance of individuals like himself, who had been endowed with the special gift of self-control. To the married estate he applied the principle of subordination by pointing out that husbands and wives surrendered to their spouses the authority over their own bodies (7:3-4). In the chapter that is devoted to this whole question we find a very difficult section, which seems to suggest that there were in Corinth certain engaged couples who proposed to live celibate lives in keeping with the apostle's personal point of view (7:36-38). Some have suggested that Paul was referring to the custom of a young man taking a young woman under his protection and both of them living together under vows of celibacy. Whatever the problem was, the apostle recognized the dangers of the situation and recommended marriage instead, wherever this seemed advisable.

Naturally, the apostle had to reckon with the problems of Christian spouses being married to pagan partners. In the social order of the Roman empire this question was bound to come up. In this matter St. Paul recommended that such couples remain married wherever this was possible. In fact, he expressed the conviction that the unbelieving spouse was sanctified by his relationship to the Christian mate, even as the children of Christian parents were sanctified by the fact that they belonged to such a family (7:14-15). Once again he reminded the church of the requirement of subordination in the question of the status of women in the church. Quite specifically, he recommended that, in the public worship service, they were to keep their hair long and their heads covered (11:6). The exercise of freedom in this direction could easily lead to serious misunderstanding in a city where courtesans went unveiled and respectable women veiled themselves outside their own homes.

In this connection we must mention the very puzzling concept of ἐξουσία as it occurs in 11:10. Normally this word is translated "authority." Since the studies of Gerhard Kittel,[23] however, published in 1920, scholars are generally agreed that here the term means a "veil." At any rate, a woman was to wear a veil, apparently in recognition of her share in the power of her husband and in his responsibilities and status. As we indicated before, angels are referred to in this context, possibly to invoke them as beings whose task it was to defend the order of creation, as Paul understood it.[24]

We note here an apparent contradiction in the demand that women remain silent at church assemblies, as given in 14:35, and the specific reference in 11:5 to women praying and prophesying. Possibly this difference can be reconciled by assuming that in the latter context Paul had in mind the fact that the members of the church often met for worship in private homes, while in the former he was making reference to public assemblies. Again, we may possibly find a solution in the fact that the Western text gives 14:34-35 at the close of the chapter. This may indicate that these particular verses originated as glosses and were inserted into the text by later scribes. At any rate, Paul was concerned for an orderly life in a community that was strongly endowed with many and various gifts of God's Spirit. This was his primary interest. Freedom in Christ, after all, is a dynamic concept that could, as Paul began to realize, destroy the very structure of community living if it turned into license.

At this point, very briefly, we give thought to the way in which both Qumran and Corinth interpreted their responsibilities in terms of everyday life. Qumran was a priestly community, devoted to the study of the Law, as we have noted. Prayers were said three times a day. Prescribed spiritual exercises were designed to help members grow in their knowledge of the mysteries of God. Members were to practice watchfulness. That is to say, they were to be ready at any moment to welcome the coming of the end. One-third of them, therefore, had to stay awake through the night, reading and studying God's law. All members were to love the sons of light and hate the children of darkness. They must observe a very strict distinction between these two realms, the kind of dualism that was reflected in the liturgy practiced by the community, with its prescribed reading of the benedictions and of the curses from the Law every time new members were received into the group. Some of the hymns which were written for and used by the community reveal much of this same sensitivity to the sharp cleavage between the spheres of light and of darkness.

Eating the common meal provided a daily opportunity to take stock of personal purity. If the description that

Josephus gives us of the Essenes applies to the Qumran community, the eating of the meal was preceded by ritual ablutions.[25] Sharing in the common meal was deemed to be a privilege of such significance that it was declared to be the equivalent of offering sacrifices in the temple at Jerusalem.[26] At the same time, this meal of the community was a constant reminder that some day all of the members would participate in such a banquet during the Messianic age, when the anointed of Aaron would preside over the assembled congregation. Disciplined eating served as training for proper participation in the Messianic banquet yet to come. The meals themselves pointed forward to the end of time, where this earthly pattern would be made to prevail for all eternity.

But there was a very sharp difference between Qumran and Corinth. There is no suggestion at all in the Qumran texts that the common meal was related in any way to the redemptive significance of an historical person,[27] as was the case in the church at Corinth. There the Eucharist was observed as part of a complete meal. It was the Lord's Supper, which he had instituted as part of his redemptive ministry. It offered an opportunity for sharing in the blessings of his life and of his death. As a matter of fact, it offered the forgiveness of sins, life and salvation even now, in view of the fact that Christ had died to give His body and shed His blood for His people.

What preceded the Lord's Supper proper was a meal which provided the opportunity to serve others on the basis of that kind of love which, as Paul pointed out especially in Chapter 13:13, surpassed both faith and hope in terms of permanent significance. Such love had the power to weld the community together because it provided the specific antidote for the kind of knowledge that tended to produce individual pride and therefore to threaten the unity of the church. The spiritual gifts that God in His Grace might pour out on this congregation were to be used to strengthen the life of the community and to win over the unbelievers or the outsiders. Here again we note a difference between the two communities under discussion. No outsider could possibly have got into the assembly at Qumran, operating as it did on the principle of exclusion. Paul, however, specifically took cognizance of this possibility in the church at Corinth. He discouraged speaking in tongues on the ground that this would not persuade the uninitiated who might casually attend religious services (14:23), all of which were open to the public.

Members of the church were to engage in prayer and to remain watchful. They were to be strong and practice courage. The devotional and liturgical life of the community shows through the references to words of prophecy, to the singing of psalms, to instruction, and to receiving a revelation (14:26). In all of these multifarious activities, Paul insisted, there was to be as little confusion as possible and a recognition of the fact that in a hierarchy of functions the utterances of prophets took precedence (14:32). The Eucharist, after the eating of a common meal, pointed forward to the return of the Lord and the resumption of the Messianic feast alluded to by the words of institution.

We cannot leave this section without a brief note on the kind of discipline that was practiced in each of these two communities. Qumran worked out a detailed and comprehensive system of fines and other forms of punishment for those who were guilty of violating the rules of the assembly (1 QS 6:23-7:25). The fines imposed varied all the way from ten days for gesticulating with the left hand in a conversation to excommunication for betraying the secrets of the community. Anyone guilty of defection was never permitted to return to formal membership in the community on the basis of a regulation that read: "No member of the community is to associate with such a person either by recognizing him as of the same state of purity or by sharing property with him. Any of the members who does so shall be liable to the same sentence; he, too, shall be expelled" (1 QS 7:24-25).

As one reads the list of punishments for various infractions of the many rules of the community, it is impossible to escape the conclusion that the discipline at Qumran was built on the principle of fear. The very thought of being expelled from the group, even for a little while, was enough to induce a feeling of dread, for it meant being separated from the very source of one's life and its significance.

By way of contrast, the church in Corinth was expected to implement the requirement of love. Discipline was by admonition. Paul was fully aware of the mutually exclusive claims of the realm of darkness and the kingdom of light. He took cognizance of the fact that it was possible to be excluded from the Christian fellowship. For that reason he warned his readers against immorality and idolatry, against drunkenness and greed, as well as robbery and theft (6:9-10). No person guilty of such practices could possibly expect to inherit the kingdom of God, he said.

He made a special point of the vice of prostitution as a direct means of severing oneself from unity with the Lord (6:16-17).

Just how he intended this basic observation to be applied, we can determine from the case of the man who was guilty of incest. Paul directed the church, as we have seen, to exclude this person from its fellowship. Yet in this very context he was quick to add his concern for the ultimate salvation of the individual under judgment. In other words, Paul was primarily concerned to impose discipline for remedial purposes. The good of the individual and of the community was uppermost in his mind. No leaven, no matter how small the lump, must be permitted to permeate and spoil this design for community (5:6).

Some commentators assume that we have the sequel to this case in Second Corinthians 2:5-11 and 7:12, the inference being that the Corinthians held a meeting of the kind suggested by the apostle and passed the sentence of expulsion. The offender repented; the Corinthians, thereafter, awaited the apostle's permission to remit the sentence. This he did, according to 2 Corinthians 2:10. Whether this view is correct or not depends on a more general understanding of the inner connections of the two epistles ascribed to Paul. Under any circumstances, we have reason enough to assert that the disciplinary measures suggested in 1 Corinthians received their impulse from a desire to inculcate love rather than to instill fear. The apostle wanted the church to remain mindful of the possibility of final redemption even when expulsion from the congregation seemed necessary for the moment.

Chapter Four

Present Dangers

So far we have considered the two communities at
Qumran and Corinth in the light of their sense of community, their respective eschatological hopes and in terms
of their interim responsibilities. We must now discuss
these two groups in terms of the dangers that each believed to constitute threats to their respective designs
for community life. Both communities were very much
aware of the fact that the end had not yet fully come,
and that, therefore, they were still living before the
consummation of all things. They had no illusions on this
point, realizing full well that they were exposed to the
hazards inherent in this situation. They reckoned with
the transcendental rift that divided the whole universe
between two hostile powers. They knew to some extent
how this rift projected itself into the life of the community and of the individual. To these matters we must
now turn.

The Dead Sea sect was very much aware of the cosmic
dualism which pitted the camp of Belial against the Prince
of Light and his hosts. These two opposing forces consisted not only of men but of angels.[28] As the sons of
light, the members of the community were sure that they
stood under attack from the Angel of Darkness. Through
this angel, says the Manual of Discipline, "even those

who practice righteousness are made liable to error; all their sin and their iniquities, all their guilt and their deeds of transgression are the result of his domination" (1 QS 3:21-22). That is why we find in the literature of this sect a rather heavy emphasis on the need to be watchful and on the necessity of studying the Law.

These angelic beings that divided the universe between themselves were conceived of as having been created by God for their respective rule. "Thou hast made us unto Thee an eternal people," says the War Scroll, "and hast cast our lot in the portion of light that we may show forth Thy truth; and from of old Thou hast charged the Angel of Light to help us. In His hand are all works of righteousness, and all spirits of truth are under his domination. But for corruption Thou hast made Belial, an angel of hostility. All his dominion is in darkness and his purpose is to bring about wickedness and guilt. All the spirits that are associated with him are but angels of destruction" (1 QM 13:9-12).

This state of affairs was soon to end; this was the hope of Qumran. Truth would prevail; of this they were not in doubt. The war against Gog and Magog would mark the close of the present era of wickedness but not the end of the world. It would last for forty years, the period of the so-called "Messianic travail," but this was bound to bring in the age of divine favor. The blueprint for this conviction is found in what is known as the Two-Column Fragment, to which two minor items are related, namely, the New Covenant and the Coming Doom.[29] There can be little question of the fact that the members of the Qumran community expected all of history to end in annihilation by fire.

In writing to the Corinthians, the apostle Paul kept in

mind that the universe was rifted. He did not hesitate
to make a clear distinction between the kingdom of God
and the realm of darkness. The very name Belial occurs
in this kind of context. "What concord hath Christ with
Belial?" Paul inquired, for example (2 Cor. 6:15). He
knew of a "god of this world," who blinded men of unbe-
lief (2 Cor. 4:4). He viewed history in terms of Christ's
ultimate victory over all His enemies. On the side of
Christ were his saints or brethren. Opposed to Him were
the unrighteous and the unbelieving. In this kind of conflict members of the church needed to manifest a high
degree of courage by spending their days in the service of
love. Some day, of course, this gigantic struggle was
bound to end. This conflict, however, could not cease
until all of God's enemies had been subjected to Christ.

This cleft in the universe projected itself into the lives
of the individual members of the community. Of that
Qumran and Corinth were both fully persuaded. The
people of Qumran believed that the Prince of Light had
the task of enlightening men's hearts, teaching them to
rely on God's mercy by an understanding of God's works
and the practice of love toward those persons who were
interested in following the truth and achieving ritual
purity. Of course, along this road the individual was
bound to encounter the opposition of the Angel of Ob-
struction, or Mastema, as he is called (CD 16:5). All this
signified that men still lived where they were exposed to
the evils of the flesh. In fact, just to belong to the flesh
meant being part of the sphere where the spirit of perver-
sion, the Angel of Darkness, ruled.[30] This angel tempted
the individual to lewdness, blasphemy, hardness of heart,
shortness of temper and insolence. The spirits who attend
the Angel of Darkness are described as having the single-

minded purpose of causing the sons of light to stumble. On this basis, apostasy was construed to be the consequence of demonic possession (CD 12:2-6). The Qumran documents, however, like I Corinthians, promise that the God of Israel and the Angel of his Truth are always ready to help the sons of light in situations of temptation (1 QS 3:24). In fact, every member of the sect was taught to believe that effective assistance in withstanding Satan could be found only with God. One of the hymns puts it like this: "Except Thou strengthen, there is no standing; except Thou rebuke, no stumbling; no affliction but Thou hast foreknown it, no salvation but by Thy will" (10:17-18).

In his correspondence with Corinth, Paul also took note of the existence of the flesh. Although he used the term "flesh" at times in a very neutral sense, he was aware of its other dimensions. The man who was guilty of incest, of living with his father's wife, was to be expelled from the community so that the lust of his flesh might be destroyed and he himself be saved. That is the way the apostle put it. Idolatry and greed were manifestations of the spirit of evil. Living in this world, the members of the new Israel faced the same sort of temptations to disobedience, immorality and idolatry to which God's ancient people at times had succumbed. Each person in the church was exposed to the danger of aligning himself with the forces that were in revolt against God. The apostle, however, could assure his readers that God was faithful, and that he would not permit anyone to be tempted beyond his capacity to resist (10:13). Like Qumran, Corinth was made aware of the eschatological dimensions of temptation.

The cosmic rift also cut through the community design

of Qumran and Corinth as they interpreted themselves
in the light of their ultimate destiny. The Qumran rules
took cognizance of various evils that threatened particularly this aspect of life. The documents of the sect describe Belial as one who was rampant in Israel, laying
three snares for the members of the community: whore-
dom, lucre, and desecration (CD 4:12ff). The community
found it necessary to discourage by heavy punishments
any manifestation of disloyalty or disobedience. There
were specific regulations against slandering one's neigh-
bor or desiring to take revenge. The worst of all evils,
of course, consisted of betraying the principles by which
the group lived (1 QS 7:22-24). This constituted treason,
no less.

We do not have enough literature from the Dead Sea
sect to know whether it ever suffered from serious schisms.
We are left in ignorance on this point also by the fact that
the documents we have are largely prescriptive rather
than descriptive. When it comes to Corinth, however, we
are in no doubt whatsoever as to the presence of certain
dangers to the life of the congregation as such. In addition
to mentioning such matters as immorality and idolatry,
both of which had troubled ancient Israel, Paul addressed
himself particularly to the problem of factions at Corinth.

We have already noted that there seems to have been
a clique in this church which thought of itself as already
living beyond the age of the final travail. Apparently
these persons were motivated by the conviction that
through baptism they already shared in the privileges of
the exalted Lord. That is why they interpreted Christian
freedom almost in terms of license, a situation which
prompted Paul to remind them that freedom was bound
to a concern for others in the congregation. He applied

this observation especially to the question of meat which had been offered to idols and could be bought on the open market (Chapter 8). To this question in casuistry those persons who boasted of having some special kind of enlightenment applied the sophistry, "An idol is nothing" (8:4). Furthermore, they asserted their personal freedom on the principle that now "anything went" (cf. 6:12). The apostle was quick to remind them that freedom was limited by the prior question of the other person's conscience (8:10). Christians were to avoid giving offense under any circumstances.

It is not inconceivable that the persons who advocated this false kind of personal liberty comprised the "Christ party" at Corinth (1:12). They may have misunderstood the significance of their baptism, construing it to be the means by which they were able to transcend history and so share in the rights and privileges of the exalted Lord. At any rate, this seems to be the reason why St. Paul moved abruptly from his reference to baptism (1:17) to the Crucifixion as the method which God had chosen to reveal His own wisdom in an event that seemed to reflect the utmost in weakness. In this way, the apostle proposed to deflate the kind of wisdom which encouraged a tendency among some of the Corinthians to sit in judgment over others, even presuming to criticize Paul himself. They were acting like self-appointed kings, unmindful of the fact that they still lived within the limitations of an everyday existence. Only rarely did the apostle resort to such stinging irony as when he took issue with this type of presumption:

> Now ye are full, now ye are
> rich, ye have reigned as kings
> without us: and I would to God

> ye did reign, that we also might
> reign with you. . . (But) we are
> made as the filth of the world,
> and are the offscouring of all
> things unto this day (4:8-13).

Some interpreters suppose that this false wisdom was actually a kind of incipient Gnosticism.[31] They rest their case almost entirely on 2:6-16. In this unit, the first section (6-9) is said to assume a belief in the myth of a Descending and Ascending Redeemer, who functioned in a way similar to the Spirit-Revealer of Gnostic speculation (10-16).

Now, we shall have to concede that this pericope contains some of the basic terminology of later Gnosticism, such as *teleioi, archontes, mysterion, pneumatikoi, psychikoi,* and "the depths of God." Moreover, verse 9 uses a quotation, possibly from the Apocalypse of Elijah, that occurs very frequently in the literature of the Gnostics. However, we can counter these items, first of all, with a notice that the apostle does not, in this entire section, nor even in its context, use the term *gnosis*. What he does discuss in terms of contrast to the proclamation of the Cross is what he himself calls "the wisdom of the world." That is to say, he does not attempt a refutation of some kind of esoteric *gnosis*. What is more, the *teleioi* of 2:6 applies to the whole congregation. It is the equivalent of the Hebrew *tamim,* or *tamimim,* which occurs in the Dead Sea scrolls (for example, at 1 QS 8:1) as a word for the members of the community as such.[32] Again, there is no reason to look beyond the Old Testament and Judaism for the source of the distinction between *pneumatikoi* and *psychikoi*. The same is true for such other expressions as "the rulers of this age," "mystery," and "the depths of

God." In fact, since the false *gnosis* at Corinth consisted in large part of a misunderstanding of eschatology, we can hardly escape the conclusion that the apostle was dealing with an aberration which was rooted in Judaism rather than in some form of Gnosticism. Gnostic speculation did not concern itself with eschatology; Jewish apocalyptic literature did.[33] The latter, most probably, also provided the quotation found at 2:9. This makes it unnecessary to assume that Paul derived this saying from sources other than Jewish ones, even though we must recognize that Judaism had come under the influence of Hellenistic patterns of thought even before the opening decade of the Christian era.[34]

We have already suggested that Apollos may have brought this fore-shortened view of the end-time to Corinth, since he had at one time been associated with the movement of John the Baptist. It is also conceivable that some of the followers of Apollos imparted these strange views from Ephesus, where there seems to have been a community of disciples devoted to the practice of John's baptism (Acts 19:4). To be sure, when Paul wrote First Corinthians, he and Apollos were of one mind. The apostle went out of his way to stress their full accord (16:12). This does not, however, preclude the possibility that in previous months or years Apollos had labored under the misconceptions described.

The Baptist, in turn, may have absorbed some of this kind of eschatology from the Qumran community. This false view may have clung to the movement even after he himself had turned his back on the faith of the Dead Sea sect to follow the God-given conviction that the hopes of the desert community were foredoomed to failure. The latter had built its view of the end-time on that under-

standing of Isaiah 40:3 which is given in the Revised
Standard Version and reads, "A voice crying, 'In the
wilderness prepare, the way of the Lord. . .'" (cf. 1 QS
8:14). By way of contrast John proclaimed the rendering
given in the Septuagint; consequently he described himself as a voice crying in the desert, "Prepare the way of
the Lord." He sent those who came to him to be baptized for the remission of their sins back into the world
to carry out the responsibilities of the end-time. Under
the guidance of its Lord the church extended this point
of view, believing that it must go out into all the world,
even into a metropolis like Corinth, to gather in the full-
ness of the Gentiles. The apostle Paul understood very
well that the church had been called into being not to
fence in its special revelation but to proclaim and share
its understanding of the mysteries of God.

Qumran, therefore, ceased to exist when Roman troops
overran the desert of Judah. Its members hid the literature of the community in caves that lay beyond the
reach of soldiers under orders to put down a rebellion.
Possibly, some of those who survived the destruction of
their tightly organized society joined the Christian church.
If they did, they must have done so on the conviction
that their newly adopted faith was that of a community
endowed with God's Spirit and created to be the true
people of the end-time, the abiding remnant of God's
Israel according to the Spirit.

Conclusion

This study has been devoted to an analysis of the concepts of unity and community as these were understood respectively by the Qumran sect in its literature and by the apostle Paul in his correspondence with the Christians at Corinth. We have seen that both communities felt a strong sense of community and at times expressed this conviction in similar terms. The church's understanding of herself as God's people, however, went beyond that of Qumran. She was ready and willing to use the Greek term ἐκκλησία of herself, thereby reminding herself that the congregation of the end-time, endowed as it was with God's Spirit, had the task of gathering in the Gentiles. Qumran never got beyond the limits of Judaism. Its members interpreted their task as that of being the true Israel rather than a new kind of community, chosen to manifest a new dimension of life.

Both Qumran and Corinth thought of themselves in terms of continuity and discontinuity with the Old Testament. St. Paul felt the discontinuity more keenly than did the Teacher of Righteousness; for the apostle was fully persuaded that the revelation given in Jesus Christ superseded that of the Torah given by angels to Moses. Both communities believed that they were living at the end of days. The Messianic hopes of Qumran, however, did not center in the return of a Saviour who had once entered history as God incarnate. They knew of no Anointed One that had died, that had been raised again from the dead, and ascended on high to assume the rule of heaven and earth until history's end. The Dead Sea sect was determined to bring in the kingdom of God by ceremonial purity and organized economic and military strength, to be used in a campaign against the sons of Belial. It looked forward to the coming of a priestly and a lay Messiah to consummate their hopes and achievements.

Until the coming of these Messiahs, life at Qumran came under rigorous discipline according to a very strict interpretation of the Law. Life in the congregation at Corinth, by way of contrast, overflowed with the impulse of God's Spirit. Both groups took temptation very seriously, on the conviction that no greater misfortune could befall an individual than separation from the community. Both were fully aware of a cosmic conflict going on between the realm of darkness and the kingdom of light. It was the conviction of the church at Corinth, however, that the decisive battle had already been won at the Crucifixion and the Resurrection. Qumran knew of no such triumph in the past. It still belonged to the old aeon. It had not yet been redeemed. It could only hope that some day salvation might be effected. Qumran, therefore, ceased to exist many centuries ago. It had nothing new to offer. Its members continued to be children of the covenant from Sinai, "which gendereth to bondage."

A comparative study, such as this, therefore, can only help us to appreciate more fully the new dimensions of God's end-time creation, the church. It was on this community that God poured out His Spirit, thereby rebuilding the tabernacle of David which had fallen into ruins, as James reminded the persons attending the first Jerusalem Council (Acts 15:16), so that the Gentiles, too, might seek the Lord and praise Him in the fellowship of prophets and apostles. To this God be all glory now and forevermore!

Notes

1. This is an allusion to Renan's famous statement that "Christianity is an Essenism which has largely succeeded." This whole matter is discussed by Krister Stendahl in *The Scrolls and the New Testament* (New York: Harper and Brothers, 1957), pp. 4, 5.

2. Romans 11:17.

3. Especially in his *Sanctorum Communio: Eine dogmatische Untersuchung zur Soziologie der Kirche*. This terminology is an application of the distinction made by Ferdinand Toennies' *Gemeinschaft und Gesellschaft* (Eng. trans.: *Fundamental Concepts of Sociology*). A further application of this difference is made by Peter L. Berger in an article entitled "The Problem of Christian Community in Modern Society," *Lutheran World*, VIII, No. 1 (June, 1960), 14-22.

4. In his *Bell. Jud.*, II, 8.5.

5. Cf. Theodor H. Gaster, *The Dead Sea Scriptures* (New York: Doubleday Anchor, 1957), p. 138.

6. Gaster, *op. cit.*, p. 310.

7. *Ibid.*, p. 119.

8. *Ibid.*, p. 65.

9. Cf. CD 6:14-19, where *lehbadal*, the technical word for separation, occurs.

10. In Books VI to VIII.

11. Cf. Shemaryahu Talmon, "The Calendar Reckoning of the Sect from the Judean Desert" in *Scripta Hierosolymitana* (Jerusalem: Magnes Press, 1958), IV, 162-69.

12. Gaster, *op. cit.*, pp. 252-53.

13. *Op. cit.*, p. 252.

14. Cf. Jacob Licht, "An Analysis of the Treatise on the Two Spirits in DSD" in *Scripta Hierosolymitana*, IV, pp. 88-

100, and also David Flusser, "The Dead Sea Sect and Pre-Pauline Christianity," *ibid.*, pp. 215-66.

15. In his interpretation, as given in the *Interpreter's Bible*, Clarence Tucker Craig points to the three possible meanings of the Aramaic expression and decides for the liturgical use as given in *Didache* 10:6.

16. Cf. Flusser, *op. cit.*, p. 227.

17. Cf. W. H. Brownlee, "John the Baptist in the New Light of the Ancient Scrolls" in *The Scrolls and the New Testament*, ed. Krister Stendahl, p. 35.

18. *Ibid.*

19. Cf. 1 Corinthians 12:3, which is included by Oscar Cullmann in a list of early formulas of faith in *Christ and Time* (Philadelphia: Westminster Press, 1950), p. 114.

20. *Bell. Jud.*, II, 8.2-13; *Antiquities*, XIII, 5.9; XVIII, 1.5.

21. *Ibid.*

22. Oscar Cullmann, *op. cit.*, p. 39.

23. G. Kittel, *Rabbinica* (Leipzig: J. C. Hinrichs, 1920), pp. 17-31.

24. Cf. Robertson-Plummer, *The First Epistle of Paul to the Corinthians* (ICC) (Edinburgh: T. & T. Clark, 1953), p. 233, for various interpretations.

25. Josephus, *Bell. Jud.*, II, 8.5.

26. Cf. Karl Georg Kuhn, "The Meal," in Stendahl, *op. cit.*, p. 68.

27. *Ibid.*, p. 78.

28. Cf. David Flusser, *op. cit.*, p. 223; also Gaster, *op. cit.*, p. 282 (1 QM 1:15).

29. Cf. Gaster, *op. cit.*, pp. 307-14.

30. Cf. Kuhn, "Temptation, Sin and Flesh" in Stendahl, *op. cit.*, p. 107.

31. This is the approach of Ulrich Wilckens, *Weisheit und Torheit* (Tuebingen: J. C. B. Mohr, 1959) and of W. Schmithals, *Die Gnosis in Korinth* (Goettingen: Vandenhoeck and Ruprecht, 1956).

32. Cf. footnote 16 above; also W. D. Davies, "Paul on Flesh and Spirit" in Stendahl, *op. cit.*, p. 179.

33. Cf. W. D. Davies, " 'Knowledge' in the Dead Sea Scrolls and Matthew 11:25-30" in *Harvard Theological Review*, XLVI (July, 1953), 113-39, for a discussion of this vital distinction. Also J. Dupont, *Gnosis: Le Connaissance Religieuse* . . . (Louvain: E. Nauwelaerts, 1949), p. 44.

34. Cf. R. McL. Wilson, "Some Recent Studies in Gnosticism" in *NTS*, VI (October, 1959), 32-44.

Selected Bibliography

ALLEGRO, J. M. *The Dead Sea Scrolls*. Harmondsworth: Penguin, 1956.

BURROWS, MILLAR. *The Dead Sea Scrolls*. New York: Viking Press, 1956.

————. *More Light on the Dead Sea Scrolls*. New York: Viking Press, 1958.

CROSS, FRANK M., JR. *The Ancient Library of Qumran and Modern Biblical Studies*. Garden City: Doubleday, 1958.

DAVIES, WILLIAM D. " 'Knowledge' in the Dead Sea Scrolls and Matthew 11:25-30," *Harvard Theological Review*, XLVI (July, 1953), 113-39.

DUPONT, JACQUES. *Gnosis: Le Connaissance Religieuse*. Louvain: E. Nauwelaerts, 1949.

DUPONT-SOMMER, ANDRÉ. *The Jewish Sect of Qumran and the Essenes*. London: Vallentine, Mitchell, 1954.

ELLIGER, KARL. *Studien zum Habakuk-Kommentar vom Toten Meer*. Tuebingen: J. C. B. Mohr, 1953.

GASTER, THEODOR. *The Dead Sea Scriptures*. New York: Doubleday Anchor, 1957.

LICHT, JACOB. *The Thanksgiving Scroll* (Hebrew). Jerusalem, 1957.

MILIK, J. T. *Ten Years of Discovery in the Wilderness of Judaea*. Vol. XXVI in *Studies in Biblical Theology*. London: SCM Press, 1959.

NOETSCHER, F. *Zur Theologischen Terminologie der Qumran-Texte*. Bonn, 1956.

RABIN, CHAIM. *Qumran Studies*. Vol. II in *Scripta Judaica*. London: Oxford University Press, 1957.

RABIN, CHAIM AND YIGAEL YADIN, eds. *Scripta Hierosolymitana*, IV. Jerusalem: Magnes Press, 1958.

Rowley, H. H. *The Zadokite Fragments and the Dead Sea Scrolls.* New York: Macmillan, 1952.

Schmithals, W. *Die Gnosis in Korinth.* Goettingen: Vanderhoeck and Ruprecht, 1956.

Stendahl, Krister, ed. *The Scrolls and the New Testament.* New York: Harper and Bros., 1957.

Sutcliffe, Edmund F. *The Monks of Qumran.* London: Burnes and Oates, 1960.

Vermes, Geza. *Discovery in the Judaean Desert.* New York: Deselee, 1956.

Wilckens, Ulrich. *Weisheit und Torheit.* Tuebingen: J. C. B. Mohr, 1959.

Wilson, R. McL. "Some Recent Studies in Gnosticism," *New Testament Studies*, No. 6 (October, 1959), 32-44.

Yadin, Yigael. *The Scroll of the War of the Sons of Light Against the Sons of Darkness* (Hebrew). Jerusalem: Bialik, 1955.